I0438853

JOY

ORIGINAL INSPIRATIONAL QUOTATIONS
by David Ragna

© Copyright 1998

ISBN: 1-58500-215-1

Synopsis

JOY is a compilation of original inspirational sayings by its author David Ragna.

This book contains a variety of quotations that encompass the entire range of everyday experiences. All age groups can find wisdom in these words.

As the author explains, "My feelings are that these are truly inspired sayings. If we but listen, we will hear God speaking to all of us in many ways. In his Glory and Love He has impressed me with these very beautifully simple, sometimes humorous, but meaningful, words of joy. This is the way He has spoken to me and that is how the book, *JOY*, was born."

"My contribution, in this endeavor, was to merely take these inspirational ideas and put them into a literary format. I also had to find the very best avenue of exposure. I feel that I have found this with 1st Books. They provide a wonderful way to touch many souls."

The author encourages all who buy this book to spread its message of love and wisdom.

Dedicated to the one I love;
My Joy..

"SERENDIPITY IS SIMPLY GOD'S HANDIWORK"

> *"WHEN FACING DIFFICULT DECISIONS, GO OUT OF YOUR MIND AND TRUST YOUR GUT"*

> "GROWING PAINS
> ARE NOT JUST
> RESERVED
> FOR THE YOUNG"

*"THE MAGIC OF
LIFE
IS SO POWERFUL,
THAT IT
SOMETIMES
BLINDS
US INTO
THINKING THAT
THERE IS NO
MAGIC IN LIFE"*

> *"IT'S VERY DIFFICULT TO DO ANYMORE THAN YOU BELIEVE YOU CAN DO"*

"THE ONLY DIFFERENCE BETWEEN WORK AND PLAY IS ATTITUDE"

> *"NOT A DEED OF HATE,*
> *NOR A DEED OF LOVE,*
> *GOES UNSEEN BY THE LORD ABOVE"*

> *"OPINIONATED
> MINDS
> ARE USUALLY
> FILLED
> TO CAPACITY"*

`

> *"YOUR ANGER IS YOUR ADVERSARIES BEST FRIEND"*

"A CHILD'S DISCIPLINE IS NEVER COMPLETE WITHOUT A HUG"

"COMPLAINING IS SIMPLY A PETITION FOR MORE TO COMPLAIN ABOUT"

"INSPIRATION GLADLY ACCEPTS THE INVITATION OF A YEARNING SOUL"

> *"THOSE WHO KNOW THAT THINGS ALWAYS WORK OUT FOR THE BEST, ALWAYS HAVE IT VERIFIED"*

> ## "IN THE GOOD OLD DAYS, WE DREAMED OF NOW"

> *"IGNORANCE MAY BE BLISS, BUT ENLIGHTENMENT IS TRULY SUBLIME"*

> *"HOW BADLY YOU WANT TO LEARN SOMETHING, IS HOW GOOD YOU'LL BECOME AT IT"*

"WHEN WE DO EVERYTHING FOR OUR CHILDREN, WE'RE REALLY TEACHING THEM HOW TO DO NOTHING FOR THEMSELVES"

> **"TO KEEP A CONFLICT ALIVE, EVERY ACTION NEEDS A REACTION"**

"WE NEED ADVERSITY TO TEMPER OUR METTLE"

*"IN GIVING
EXPECT
NOTHING IN
RETURN
AND IN RETURN
YOU'LL
NEVER BE
DISAPPOINTED"*

"TO KEEP A MARRIAGE HEALTHY, PRACTICE THE DAILY PREVENTATIVE MAINTENANCE OF UNCONDITIONAL LOVE"

"TAKE LIFE A LITTLE SLOWER; FOR THE MORE YOU HURRY THE SOONER IT'S OVER"

"SINCE YOU'RE THE ONLY ONE REALLY FEELING IT, WHAT'S THE POINT OF BEING ANGRY?"

*"SADLY, SADNESS
LEFT TO
ITS OWN
ACCORD,
CONTINUES
TO BEGET
SADNESS"*

> ## *"RESULTS RESULT FROM REPETITION"*

*"THE BETTER YOU
FEEL
THE BETTER
YOU'LL LOOK,
THE BETTER YOU
LOOK
THE BETTER
YOU'LL FEEL"*

> *"COMPLEXITY IS MADE UP OF MANY SIMPLE THINGS"*

> *"DESIRE
> IS THE SEED
> OF CREATION"*

> *"SUBJECTIVITY IS REALLY THE ONLY REALITY WE KNOW"*

"THERE'S DAY AND NIGHT BETWEEN THOSE WHO ALWAYS TRY TO DO WHAT'S RIGHT, AND THOSE WHO ALWAYS THINK WHAT THEY DO IS RIGHT"

> *"THOSE THAT
> WORSHIP GOLD
> NEVER HAVE
> ENOUGH,
> AND THOSE THAT
> DON'T
> HAVE ALL THEY
> NEED"*

*"THE FIRST THING
YOU NEED
TO DO TO REPAIR
A
BROKEN
RELATIONSHIP
IS TO FIX
YOURSELF"*

"THE POWER OF MONEY STRENGTHENS THE STRONG AND WEAKENS THE WEAK"

"ARGUING IS THE PERFECT WAY TO ACHIEVE THE OPPOSITE OF WHAT YOUR TRYING TO ACHIEVE"

"AGGRESSION AND ASSERTIVENESS ABHOR ANGER"

"THE ONLY TIME YOU REALLY HAVE A PROBLEM IS WHEN YOU LEAVE GOD OUT OF THE EQUATION"

*"WHEN YOU'RE
ALWAYS
TRYING TO
CHANGE
YOUR MATE INTO
SOMEONE
BETTER,
YOUR MATE MAY
TRY TO MAKE A
CHANGE
FOR SOMEONE
BETTER"*

> *"SELF DOUBT*
> *PLUGS*
> *THE FONT*
> *OF CREATIVITY"*

"CRITICISM WAS CREATED BY GOD TO BE USED ONLY ON YOURSELF AND OTHERS WHO REQUEST IT"

"THOSE THAT TAKE MORE THAN THEY GIVE, ALWAYS END UP WITH THE LEAST IN THE END"

"NO ONE EVER
STRAYS SO
FAR THAT THEY
ARE
LOST FOREVER;
FOR THE GOOD
LORD
IS ETERNALLY
PATIENT"

"*DISSATISFACTION ALWAYS SEEKS A NEW ATTRACTION*"

*"IN AN ARGUMENT
BOTH SIDES
ALWAYS
AGREE THAT THE
OTHER SIDE IS
WRONG,
AND OF COURSE
TO SOME
DEGREE
THEY'RE ALWAYS
RIGHT"*

"INSECURITY ALWAYS HIDES BEHIND INTIMIDATION"

> *"CHILDREN ALWAYS OBSERVE THEIR PARENTS MORE THAN THEY LISTEN TO THEM"*

"NOTHING IS MORE HUMBLING THAN STUMBLING"

> *"THE BEST TIME
> TO
> GET EVEN WITH
> YOUR
> TRANSGRESSOR
> IS NEVER;
> THEIR SUSPENSE
> IS
> YOUR REVENGE"*

"IF YOU'RE CONSTANTLY LOOKING FOR YOUR MATE'S MISTAKES, YOU'LL PROBABLY FIND THAT THEIR BIGGEST ONE WAS MEETING YOU"

*"CENSORSHIP IS
WHEN
THE PEOPLE
YOU'VE
GIVEN POWER
TO,
TAKE IT AWAY
FROM YOU,
IN AN ATTEMPT
TO PROTECT
YOU FROM
YOURSELF"*

*"FINANCIAL
SUCCESS
HAS ACTUALLY
VERY
LITTLE TO DO
WITH A
SUCCESSFUL
LIFE"*

> *"JUST BY THE VERY NATURE OF THINGS, THE GUILTY CAN NEVER GO UNPUNISHED"*

"RESOLVING A CONFLICT IS SOMETIMES VERY DIFFICULT, BUT IT IS ALSO ALWAYS VERY SIMPLE"

> "IN AN ENLIGHTENED SOCIETY, THE IDEA IS NOT TO PUNISH THE GUILTY, BUT TO PROTECT THE INNOCENT"

> "BEHIND HATRED, YOU'LL ALWAYS FIND FEAR"

*"SOMETIMES WE
NEED TO
HAVE OUR BACKS
AGAINST
THE WALL
BEFORE WE
CAN MOVE
FORWARD"*

"IN REALITY, CHILDREN LOVE THE DISCIPLINE THEY DISLIKE"

> *"TO TRULY BECOME CLOSER TO GOD, WE NEED A LITTLE MORE REVELRY AND A LITTLE LESS REVERENCE"*

> *"DISAGREEABLE
> PEOPLE
> ARE THOSE WHO
> HAVEN'T YET
> LEARNED
> TO AGREE TO
> DISAGREE"*

> *"THE FABRIC OF UNHAPPINESS IS SEWN TOGETHER WITH THREADS OF SERIOUSNESS"*

"ACCOMPLISHMENTS ARE FORGED WHEN YOU TEMPER YOUR TEMPER"

"TO SEE HOW GREEN THE GRASS IS ON THE OTHER SIDE OF THE FENCE, TAKE A LEAP OVER, THEN TAKE A LOOK BACK"

> "FEAR IS FICKLE
> INDEED;
> IT ONLY REMAINS
> WITH
> YOU UNTIL YOU
> LOOK IT IN THE
> EYE"

"HURTING YOUR
MATE'S FEELINGS
IS THE SAME AS
STEPPING
ON YOUR OWN
FOOT"

"BEFORE YOU FORM YOUR OWN OPINIONS, LEARN FROM THE MORE EXPERIENCED, THEN FORM YOUR OWN OPINIONS"

Thank you for taking part
in this adventure of Love.

It is my hope that these
words brought some
joy into your life.

Anyone wishing to contact
me may do so at:
DRGodlvsU2@excite.com

**May God bless you
and I hope we will
meet again in future
books**

David Ragna

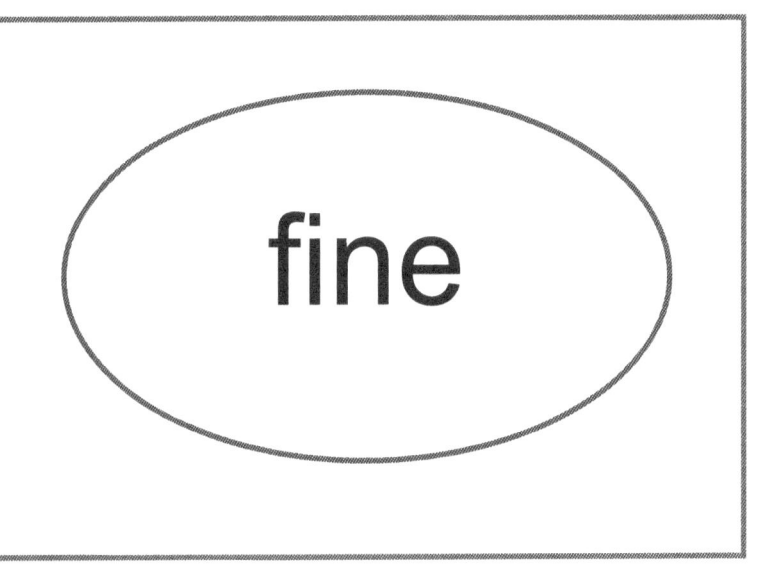

About the Author

Dave Ragna was born in 1937 and has lived his whole life in the Midwestern part of the United States.

He has been happily married for 40 years and has six lovely children. Dave and his spouse also have sixteen grandchildren and one great-grandchild.

He loves music and has done some composing and performing locally.

Dave feels that God has inspired him to write these sayings and they can apply to anybody at various times of their life. "If just one person, he says, finds Gods peace from these words, then the purpose of writing this book is truly satisfied."